Talking Flowers:

How to Become Wealthy Selling Floral Images

Images and Inscriptions upon Flower Petals

Today they are called "Talking Flowers". They allow us to express our feelings without saying a word.

In the early 2000's a unique new service emerged on the American floral market - the application of congratulatory words and images inscribed upon the petals of live flowers.

This innovative business idea immediately received a positive response in society and became high in demand by consumers. A simple inscription on a flower petal transforms any floral arrangement or bouquet into a unique original product.

This service was unheard of previously, and was therefore, part of a new direction in floral design, which would radically change the course of the entire floral market in the United States.

Consequently, this type of flower decoration has gained popularity among advertisers, since it was now possible to capture any image on the petal of a flower, even a company logo.

Currently, the worldwide sales estimates of this newly discovered business exceed over $300 million US a year. Each year the technology necessary for this task becomes less and less complex, allowing for better, more affordable, quality application of images on the flower petals, which makes it an increasingly popular idea for small businesses, and one which has become particularly sought after not only in large cities, but also in small towns around the world.

companies that sell them. Undoubtedly, printing and transferring images onto flowers is a truly promising business idea with excellent commercial potential.

Capturing consumer's attention with flowers with a personal image or inscription is easy, since the very thought of purchasing inscribed flowers is significantly more attractive than purchasing just an ordinary bouquet.

Inscribed flowers can be used as decorations for weddings, birthdays and anniversaries, as well as for conducting corporate public relations campaigns.

Color branding for enterprises is also possible, since the petals can be decorated with images of any complexity, from the company logo to the invitation to a corporate meeting or even an invitation to participate in a government function such as an election. It's original and incredibly beautiful. There are no boundaries to where flowers can be incorporated, and therefore this market is simply enormous and like a flower, guaranteed to grow.

Characteristics of Previous Technologies

"Talking Flowers" appeared on the market more than 10 years ago, but the technological aspects of the service became available only relatively recently. Why?

Initially, the technology of "Talking Flowers" was used by American specialists, who started Speaking Roses International. Currently, this company is working on developing a worldwide franchising network.

Special printers that printed images directly on the flowers, roses in particular, were the principle form of application. The technology was instantly in high demand and during the first year of its implementation "Talking Flowers" could be bought in the United States, the Netherlands, Australia, Kenya, Kuwait, the U.A.E., Saudi Arabia, Bahrain, Bangkok, Lebanon, India, Singapore, South Africa, Portugal and Spain.

What is the Secret of Success of this Innovative Idea?

Its popularity is quite simple to explain - people often resort to flowe a sign of affection for loved ones, relatives, friends and colleagues. T flower market is indeed enormous, but just one single flower with a pleasant inscription or an exclusive image is a unique gift and, of cou an incredibly effective tool for implementing an advertising or marke campaign.

We should also note that this segment of the market will remain rela competition free for at least the next ten years, which allows for the possibility of turning a virtual business idea into a truly viable and significant revenue source with relatively few competitors for some t to come.

Imagining the potential flower market volume for flower petals with images and inscriptions is quite easy. To judge this, one can simply tal look at the number of flower shops that sell bouquets daily and in ver large numbers.

Every day, in every city, there are parties, anniversaries, birthdays and corporate events that always require bouquets of flowers. In addition, millions of people give flowers to each daily. But now the gift of flowe can be not only beautiful, but also original, touching, unique, memora and personal. "Talking flowers" can transform any event into a beautif and fantastic personal celebration.

Naturally, your probably wondering - how much would this delightful floral presentation cost me? You will probably be surprised to know th today the price of inscriptions on flower petals rarely exceeds $1 US.

As far as the images go, it mainly depends upon the set of colors, the complexity of the image, etc., but, in spite of these small "complexities" the final cost of the service is, on average, under $5 US.

It is easy to see the economic potential to be gained when one multipli these figures with the already massive world wide market for flowers. I the end it becomes quite clear that selling flowers with images and inscriptions on the petals is not just an interesting idea - but an idea tha time has come, that will allow for multi-million dollar profits for the

At the international HortiFair in Amsterdam "Talking Flowers" received the award for the most outstanding achievement in the world of floral technologies. The technology became one of the TOP innovative and attractive ideas for the development of the floral market, and has become in high demand worldwide.

The technology of printing directly on the flowers required advanced know-how, but it entailed a considerable number of distinctive difficulties. In particular, inscription application required the purchasing of expensive and sophisticated equipment, as well as delivering flowers directly to printers or installing equipment in the stores. All of that was not always justified, especially not for retail chains.

It is important to remember that transporting flowers is not easy, since it requires special cars and experienced staff, and all of this combined reflects on the value of each flower and significantly reduces the mobility of the business.

As a result the cost of image application was high - about 3 to 4 dollars per image for a wholesale client. This created problems for the realization of this business for small companies with a limited budget.

In order for a shop owner to open and run their own "Talking Flower" business in the United States, it was first necessary to obtain the franchise license and special equipment from Speaking Roses International, which required them to pay at least $400000 US.

In addition, a significant disadvantage of this technology is the lack of full-color image printing, i.e. one can only print in one color of the client's choice.

With all these disadvantages only a few companies decided it was cost effective.

Subsequently, more affordable alternatives emerged on the market - in particular, Chinese ink-jet printers that would print in full color directly on the flowers. Celestial Empire amazed the industry with their cheap analogue printing devices, which subsequently became in high demand, but not all went as smoothly as many would have hoped.

Chinese printers created images of excellent quality and were noticeably faster than the equipment of Speaking Roses International, but the technology had its drawbacks.

For a start, the cost of one unit is $3000 US, minus supplies. It is inexpensive compared to what the founder of this technology offered, but still far from cheap. In addition, the printing process is not easy, since it is a stationary device that operates relatively slowly and requires application of a special gel solution onto the flower petals that can only be purchased in China.

The printer can be loaded with up to 3 flowers at a time, and printing each of them can take up to 7 minutes. In addition to that, in order to achieve the highest quality of the images, it is necessary to sort the flowers by the size of the bud and the height of the stem.

The probability of defect is about 25% (flowers with incorrectly printed images will have to be disposed of). Therefore, image application is a process that remains lengthy and expensive (the typical cost is $3 US or more), clearly inconvenient and uniquely unpredictable in terms of productivity. Plus, the software was only available in Chinese.

What can be concluded from all this information? The reality of a "Talking Flower" business model with a stable revenue stream is under question. One cannot work like that, and the cost of the final product does not meet the expectations of not only the flower buying public, but also of private and wholesale customers, as well as flower shop owners.

New Floral Jet Technology

The solution to the problem of multi-tasking, business mobility and high labor costs in relation to inscribed flowers came from Japan. The Japanese have developed a new technology, that they call Floral Jet, which they subsequently sold to a company in Europe. The task of simplifying "Talking Flower" technology and making it more cost-effective was completed with perfection.

The new technology implements the method of printing not directly on the flower, but on a sublime (12 micron) completely transparent elastic film attached to a solid base. Presently, Floral Jet Film is manufactured in Europe.

Format - standard A4. Not so long ago the film became freely available for sale, and is offered in standard packs of 10, 50 and 400 sheets. You can purchase Floral Jet Film here:

www.amazon.com/gp/product/B00FPJ8HP6

www.amazon.com/gp/product/B00FPJ6A4Q

www.amazon.com/gp/product/B00FOOIMIO

The material is completely safe for people and does not have a negative effect on the appearance of the living flower. The principle difference of this film from the previous technology is the possibility of applying images with the help of an ordinary ink-jet printer.

There is no need to request or purchase rights for manufacture or to order incredibly expensive equipment while worrying about possible defects.

Now, in order to manufacture "Talking Flowers" one only needs to purchase the film, a computer and a regular ink-jet printer. The printing process is no different than printing with plain paper.

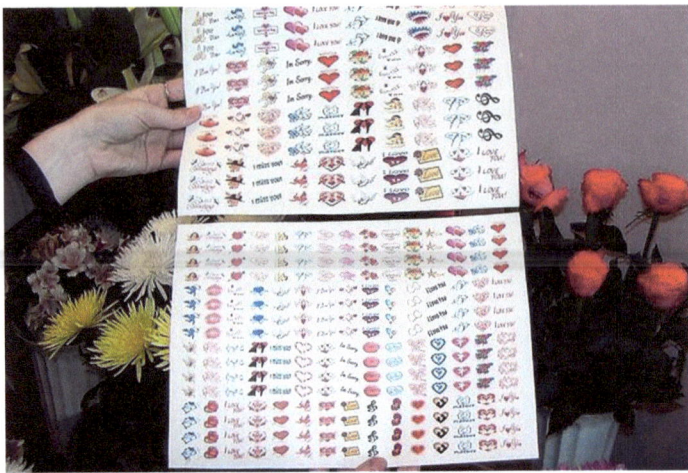

During printing the image is applied onto a super-thin film-sticker. It easily removes from the base, and afterwards it can easily be attached onto the petal (see video at youtu.be/3-ZrSBqG96Q).

Floral Jet Film Material is unique, since upon application of the image onto the flower the material is not visible on the flower even with careful examination from up close - one can only see a clear colorful image.

The image and text options are endless. Wishes, greetings, invitations, pictures and photos can be printed.

One sheet of floral film is enough for 120 medium-size images or 240 small-size images that can be transferred onto a flower at any time.

Transferring images onto the flower is simple, taking only 5 to 10 seconds, and requiring no special training. All you have to do is simply pick up a printed sheet of the film, cut the selected image out with scissors and paste it on the petal. The film is compatible with any flowers and can be used to decorate not just roses, but also lilies, tulips and other flowers.

As soon as color film emerged on the mass production market, it was instantly met with a large amount of skepticism. Many argued that such "stickers" will look unnatural, but they were proven wrong. Thanks to the fact that the film is so thin, and thanks to its special composition, it does not glare in the sun and is completely transparent. In addition, it also preserves the texture of the petals.

If you look at the flower closely, it will seem as if it always had the inscription or image on its petals! Thus, natural look of the product has been preserved, and the production has become much easier, allowing us to utilize the new technology in the mass production market.

Every sheet of the film is lightweight, transparent and universal, and will fit 180 images on average.

It is possible to sell images as entire printed sheets (A4) and separate sheets of stickers with various themes. Printing can simply be implemented on any standard ink-jet printer.

You can also easily master silk screen printing that will allow for application of striking inscriptions and images in gold, silver or fluorescent colors that glow in the dark.

All of this clearly demonstrates that the new technology not only eliminates the deficiencies of printing directly onto flowers, but also provides plenty of other opportunities for more daring and innovative ideas in floral design.

Key Advantages of the New Technology

Taking everything described above into consideration, we can conclude that the key advantages of Floral Jet technology can be summarized as follows:

1. No risk involved

You do not have to risk losing your money, calculate the probability of defected products, use special gels, etc., since now the image can be transferred onto the flowers immediately prior to their sale. Foil tightly sticks to the petal and can be easily removed, if necessary, without damaging the flower and then reapplied. Right there and then, the customer can select an image that is the most suitable for a particular event (birthday, wedding, corporate function, etc.) and the flower that the image should be applied to.

2. Work from home

You do not have to purchase expensive equipment or organize transportation of fragile flowers. If you have a computer, an ink-jet printer and Floral Jet Film supplies, you can get started with the work at any time. There is no need to rent extra space, since you can work from home or at your store.

3. Quick and easy

An image can be applied onto the flower in less than 10 seconds. All you need to do is to cut out the selected image, separate the film from the base and transfer the sticker onto the flower. All this can be done without any special equipment.

4. High profitability

The cost of each image applied onto a flower with Floral Jet Film material is as low as $ 0.07 US. Even if you sell images for as little as $1 US (although the market price average is $3 US), your income will be 15 times greater than the total applied cost!

5. Mobility

Thanks to the invention of the Floral Jet Technology the "Talking Flower" business has become extremely mobile. For example, fifty thousand images that weigh no more than 11 pounds can easily fit into a regular plastic bag! This product can easily be sent by courier service or mail, or delivered to retail outlets that sell natural flowers.

6. Versatility

Images can be applied on any area of the flower, even on the inside of the petals or the inside of the bud - for example, on a rose bud. Just imagine the incredible surprise that this rose will bring when it finally blooms!

Commercial Potential of Floral Jet Technology

You will not have to think twice about who to sell the film with printed images to, as your customer base are already established flower enterprises and any retail outlets that sells natural flowers.

Their owners will be definitely interested in the opportunity to make their product stand out when compared to the products of their competitors, and applying images to flowers will be an excellent way to achieve this opportunity. In addition, the price of a flower with a printed image will increase profit from $2 US to $5 US, which will bring substantial additional income to retailers. Therefore, your prospective clients will be definitely interested in buying images that are ready to be transferred onto flowers.

The commercial potential of Floral Jet is obvious - this is a business with a multi-million dollar turnover. Once you have mastered this user-friendly technology, you can set up a profitable production facility at your house and have the potential for a "home-based business" that has already managed to prove its viability in real market conditions.

Printing images on floral film is an inexpensive and simple business activity that will take you to a new niche of the enormous floral market that is just beginning to emerge worldwide.

The start-up costs for this business involve only advertising and purchasing of Floral Jet Film.

How Much Can You Earn? Expenses and Profit.

The prevailing wholesale price of applying one image onto the flower averages out to $1 US (when ordering prints for 10000 flowers). That is how much manufacturers and sellers of flowers pay for application of images when employing the direct printing method.

Individual wholesale prices for orders for most flower shops and companies involved in advertising activities are $1.5 US for one image.

Cost for an exclusive order for companies specializing in organizing election campaigns, corporate events, weddings, parties and presentations range from $2 US to $5 US per image.

Thus, the cost for direct image application onto a flower is on average $3 US per flower.

The net cost of images depends on the purchase price of the floral film. The manufacturer of Floral Jet Film sells it in standard packs of 10, 50 and 400 sheets that vary in price per sheet depending on the size of the order.

It goes without saying that it is more cost-effective for a business to select an optimal package of 400 sheets, as the price for one sheet of film averages out to be the lowest. The most economical option for businesses implementing the new technology will be the purchase of a pack of 50 sheets, and/or a pack of 10 sheets as a simple trial package that may be used for familiarizing oneself with the technology and completing first trial orders.

Since this book is aimed at people who want to start their own business and earn maximum income, we will consider, as an example, what is entailed when purchasing a pack of 400 sheets.

Example:

So, when buying a pack of 400 Floral Jet film sheets at $2800 US, the price of one sheet equates to $7 US.

One sheet allows for the printing of between 120 to 240 images. On average, one sheet produces 180 images.

The prices for outdated direct color services are (on average $3 US per flower), with one image costing only $1 US. So you not only leave rivals far behind, but also get a 1300% increase in income!

Since on a single sheet of Floral Jet Film you can print an average of 180 images, one printed sheet will make you $180 US.

Here is the provisional amount of the potential income from the sale of 400 sheets with images, without taking into account advertising costs:

1. Purchasing costs for 400 sheets of Floral Jet Film - $2800 US;

2. Cost of ink-jet cartridges for 400 sheets (set of 2) - up to $100 US;

3. Minimum sales proceeds from 400 sheets (72000 ready images) - $72000 US;

Total net income amounts to $69100 US.

Printing of 400 sheets (72000 images on average) will take 16 hours, and the realization time of this amount of images ranges from a few days to 1 month (and this only pertains to retail and distribution to flower shops).

As you can see, the new technology is not only promising, and has a number of indisputable advantages, but also is extremely profitable.

Who are your Potential Customers and How Would you Go about Advertising your Product

Floral Markets: Flower Shops

Retailers and wholesalers, as well as flower growers, buy images with one purpose - to promote sales in order to obtain significant additional income. Every town, even a small one, has multiple shops that daily sell a lot of flowers. Image application allows the seller to not only make greater profit while selling the same amount of flowers at their point of sale, but also to motivate the buyer to come back next time. The buyer will prefer to come back to that particular establishment, because it is there that they can buy not just flowers, but an original gift that by far deserves to cost a touch more than simple flowers.

You will supply the flower shop with A4 sheets with the popular printed images with various themes (love, holidays, weddings, celebrations, etc), convince the seller (it's easy) to start offering the new exciting services (even if paid in installments) and place advertising for the offered services at the point of sale.

The rest is pretty simple. The buyer comes to the store, notices your advertising and inquires about it, at which point the seller offers the buyer to view the catalog with images that you had left with them. The customer selects the image they liked the best, for example, the inscription that reads "Happy Birthday" or "I love you".

The seller then uses scissors to cut the selected image out (roughly along the contours), separates it from the base and applies it onto the flower selected by the buyer. The film instantly sticks to the petal - all the work is done in just 5-10 seconds, and the store makes a significantly greater profit in comparison with selling simple flowers.

It's quick, beautiful, and, of course, profitable!

Everybody who will see the "Talking Flowers" outside of the store will absolutely love them and will take an interest in this service. Thus, you will get some of the best visual advertising ever, and it will be free. "Talking Flowers" will naturally become more and more popular, and will attract more new regular customers to the store.

Retail Chains: Supermarkets and Shops

You can sell images as sets of stickers by supplying them to any retail chain - from gasoline stations to supermarkets. Store owners are always interested in expanding the assortment of their goods, and buyers are always looking for new exciting products. That way, store owners are guaranteed additional stable income, and buyers are guaranteed to receive satisfaction from purchasing a new product.

You will have to create colorful packaging with a few images inside (for example, 3 stickers with different designs with a "Happy Birthday" theme) along with the instructions on how to apply the images onto a flower.

Create a catchy package, conduct a few promotional events - and you are a manufacturer of a new unique product!

To ensure this kind of cooperation, all you have to do is convince the retail outlet representative to accept a new product for sale.

It is often enough to simply show them the "Talking Flowers", but in some cases they might need extra motivation.

Forms of motivation might be, for example, a substantial discount on the purchase of the first batch of stickers, installment payment and substantial proof in favor of the new type of product (a new direction in the market, lack of competition, the high demand in flower shops, etc.).

The success of the enterprise depends on your product and on how you promote it. The best time to start selling the product is during the holidays (Christmas, New Year, Valentine's Day, etc.).

On top of that, you will have absolutely no competition, and it is quite a significant motivation to start a business that provides for the most favorable conditions for the businesses development!

Photo Studios

Cooperation with photo studios opens even more new opportunities. In this case, the focus is on printing the photos of individual customers on the flowers. With good advertising this service will become extremely popular, since it is hard to find a more personal gift than a flower with a photo of a couple or a loved one.

Advertising Companies

Flower branding is not yet popular, the main reason being is that this segment of the market has not been explored well enough. Provided you can occupy this niche in a timely fashion, the continuous large orders for logos, emblems for pre-election campaigns, photographs of company staff members, etc., are guaranteed to bring you a stable income.

Catering and Wedding Planning Companies

In any area where the flowers are a gift, accessory or decoration (concerts, weddings, corporate events, etc.), they can be decorated with congratulatory inscriptions and images. For that reason, any wedding provider, hotel, concert hall, exhibition hall and educational institution are potential clients that could form a stable market for realization of ready floral images.

Online Trading

Almost all flower shops also offer online services. This is a clear indicator that trading of real goods on the internet is becoming increasingly more popular. In a matter of minutes, buyers can find exactly what they are looking for while at home in front of their computers, and stores can save considerable amounts of money on increasing consumer demand in regards to rental of retail space.

People can create their own website or social networking page, and use them to promote and sell their products virtually anywhere. When providing your services online, you can find customers not only in your city, but pretty much anywhere in the world. Thanks to daily quick delivery services, your product will reach the customer within just a few days.

Since your product is compact and weighs very little, it can be sent in envelopes via regular mail. Plus, online you can present the client with the most extensive assortment of images, ranging from the most popular to the most exclusive ones. The photos of flowers with inscriptions and pictures that were already applied onto their petals will look the best.

In addition, you can make excellent sales, partnering with major online stores. In this case you do not even have to create your own web site.

Internet is an easy way to find potential customers and an excellent opportunity to increase sales. It will work for you 24 hours and 7 days a week!

Image Making Technology

Image making and application of images on the floral film is done in one of two ways: printing with an ink-jet printer or silk screening (screen printing).

To print images on Floral Jet Film you will need to use a regular ink-jet color printer with vertical sheet loading (loading from the top). Printers with horizontal loading (loading from the bottom), for example, some

Epson or HP printers, can damage the film, as they are not designed for use with thin materials.

Your home business will not succeed without a large range of different ready inscriptions and pictures (Valentine cards, wishes, greetings and much more) - all of which must be present in your catalog.

Where Can I Find Images? You can create them yourself, find them on the Internet, order them from a graphic designer or use your client's own images. To print images you can use any graphics editor (not necessarily the most powerful one).

You will create a printing layout in the editor - an A4 sheet with the selected images. Creating the layout will only take a few minutes, and printing of one single sheet - 1-2 minutes (depending on the speed of the printer).

Thus, in just 1 hour, you can print no less than 3000 images of the best quality, and in money terms it equals to at least $3000 US!

You can print pictures, inscriptions and even photos of any color, depending on how far your imagination can take you. Ink-jet printers will not allow you to print in white ink, and therefore, contrast ratio of the images will depend on the type and color of the flower petals. Images will turn out the best if applied onto flower petals of brighter shades.

For this reason, ink-jet printing is not recommended for very dark flowers, for instance, for dark red roses.

In this case, using silk screening method would be much more efficient, since it allows for application of gold, silver and white colors onto petals. Besides, with silk screening you can create inscriptions that glow in the dark with the help of fluorescent colors.

Screen printing process is not complicated. Nowadays, you can purchase kits that are designed specifically for this purpose, on the Internet (in particular, sets for printing on clothes that cost about $40 US per set).

The key to creating layouts for screen printing templates is the need to work separately with each color, that is, the need to work with layers. A few layouts are created and then sent to the printer. This process will take several minutes on average for each type of image and will depend on the selected color palette.

All the necessary information and instructions on silk screening and using special printing sets can be easily found on the Internet.

Screen printing usually involves from one to three different shades. Using a greater number of colors is expensive and does not always justify the time spent.

Screen printing in gold and silver colors is ideal for creating greeting inscriptions and images on the flowers of darker shades.

You can master screen printing at a later stage of your business, since this method is more complicated than ink-jet printing and is not a prerequisite for starting this business venture. Over time, you can easily learn this method and extend the range of the offered products by introducing this new technology.

Any graphic editor will enable you to create not just "standard" sketches from your image catalog, but also to take personal, exclusive and more expensive orders, extending the range of your services and thereby sufficiently increasing the profitability of your business.

Marketing and Advertising

"Talking flowers", or, in particular, the images on Floral Jet Film, is a unique and absolutely new product. Therefore, in order to promote your business, you will need to not only consider the price policy, but also to advertise your business.

Since it is highly unlikely that you exhibit the qualities of the genius of marketing Mark Zuckerberg, or the talent of persuasion of legendary Steve Jobs, you should remember - prior to investing money in your own business - that any product needs to be advertised. Otherwise, it will simply remain unnoticed.

The main cause of failure of many, even the most promising, projects, is trying to save money on advertising. Neither you, nor your customers will be completely satisfied until the average consumer will know that this product - stickers for flowers - will make it possible for you to decorate your ordinary flowers and make them more attractive, unique, truly beautiful and eloquent - the true works of art!

Marketing specialists claim that you can interest the target consumer by attracting their attention even for a few seconds. Create your style, make promotional materials, come up with a proper business proposal, stimulate interest by offering giveaways. Giving away just one flower with a beautiful image can be the starting point for the future success of your business.

You will need to use a different method to attract remote clients. In this case, one of the best promotional tools is a video presentation. You do not have to offer a "how-it-is-done movie". You can simply show your audience the results of your work that were used to decorate an event. You should deliver ready-to-use flower stickers in a stylish packaging with your logo and attach a quality business card. Such attention to detail will improve the image of the manufacturer and will create, in the client's subconscious, the image of a reliable and responsible partner that is exclusively dedicated to creating a quality product.

We can reaffirm the importance of marketing by simply quoting Mark Twain: "Many a small thing has been made large by the right kind of advertising".

How to Start the Business

For this business all you need to have is a basic computer, a color ink-jet printer and Floral Jet film material.

For more effective business, it is better to select the 400-sheet packaging, since, in this case, the price for 1 sheet of Floral Jet Film will be the lowest and your profits will be the highest. A simple calculation shows that, upon realization of this quantity (including all expenses) your net profit could reach around $70000 US.

A more economical option is to start your business with a 50- sheet packaging of Floral Jet Film. In this case, due to the higher sheet price, production profitability will be somewhat lower, but the profit will still equal to at least $8500 US.

If you would like to at first give this business a try, you can start by purchasing just 10 sheets of film. In this case, your income will equal approximately $1500 US.

After purchasing Floral Jet Film supplies, you will need to master the technology - and it is very simple. You will just have to learn to create printing templates on the computer and to apply images onto the flowers (each Floral Jet Film package contains the detailed instructions).

Learn how to work with the software that will help you create the templates. The hours spent on learning will later save you a considerable amount of time on production of original images and their printouts.

The key points are: creating templates for printing, scaling, rational layout of images on a sheet.

Please note that because of the small scale, not every image can be displayed correctly on a flower. Therefore, you should not take on the work that requires complex and voluminous pictures (series of photos from events, multiple poetry lines, etc.).

Practice the technique of applying the printed image on the flower, so that in the future it would be easy for you to demonstrate how to apply the film properly and what needs to be done if the sticker was applied to the flower unevenly.

In the future you can also learn silk screen printing (screen printing). That way you will be able to work with a larger assortment of flowers and, therefore, will increase the number of potential customers and the profit from each transaction.

You may also want to review the conditions in your region or town and find out how often specific events take place. This will help you create a catalog of popular images, prepare relevant samples and put them on sale.

Think about how you plan to work with clients. There are no universal strategies, and therefore you should find a reference point for creating a relevant and compelling advertising campaign. You can use attractive promotional materials and create the most appropriate for particular customers cooperation plans (discounts for wholesale customers, bonuses for retail buyers, etc.), thereby adding an increasing number of potential buyers of finished products to the list of your loyal customers.

It is important to conduct in-person meetings, as it is not always possible by means of the Internet or phone to clearly demonstrate all the advantages of your product, explain the benefits of its use and, of course, to show the perks of direct cooperation with the manufacturer, that is - you.

Create a colorful catalog, a video presentation, visually compelling samples, in other words, make your work look good and beautiful and it will increase your chances of sales and will make your products successful and popular.

Tools for Starting your Business:

We have prepared for you all the necessary tools so that you could set up and run your business as quickly as possible. You can download them at no charge at all by clicking on this link: **www.floraljet.com/tools.html**

Good luck in your business!

www.ingramcontent.com/pod-product-compliance
Lightning Source LLC
Chambersburg PA
CBHW041622180526
45159CB00002BC/979